Meditation is Powerful

Other Greer Allica books
available from Penguin

Meditation is Easy

Easy Steps to Healing

Greer Allica

Meditation is Powerful

The power of thought to change your life

Penguin Books

Penguin Books Australia Ltd
487 Maroondah Highway, PO Box 257
Ringwood, Victoria 3134, Australia
Penguin Books Ltd
Harmondsworth, Middlesex, England
Penguin Putnam Inc.
375 Hudson Street, New York, New York 10014, USA
Penguin Books Canada Limited
10 Alcorn Avenue, Toronto, Ontario, Canada M4V 3B2
Penguin Books (NZ) Ltd
Cnr Rosedale and Airborne Roads, Albany, Auckland, New Zealand
Penguin Books (South Africa) (Pty) Ltd
24 Sturdee Avenue, Rosebank, Johannesburg 2196, South Africa
Penguin Books India (P) Ltd
11, Community Centre, Panchsheel Park, New Delhi 110 017, India

First published by Penguin Books Australia Ltd 2001

10 9 8 7 6 5 4 3 2

Design by David Altheim, Penguin Design Studio
Cover photograph courtesy of photolibrary.com
Typeset in 9.75/17 pt Trade Gothic Light by Post Pre-press Group, Brisbane, Queensland
Printed and bound in Australia by McPhersons Printing Group, Maryborough, Victoria

National Library of Australia
Cataloguing-in-Publication data:

Allica, Greer.
    Meditation is powerful.

    ISBN 0 14 100054 6.

    1. Meditation. I. Title.

158.12

www.penguin.com.au

To George,
To Rob,
the angels who brought the winds of change
and taught me about love and forgiveness.
I love you both.

Acknowledgements

Special thanks to my editor, Kirsten Abbott, for her sensitive understanding of the material, helpful suggestions and enthusiasm for the project.

To Julie Gibbs, who had the vision to appreciate and accept what I wanted to share – thank you.

To Carol K. Anthony, Carol Bridges, and Louise Hay – my gratitude for their wise thoughts that have guided me on my journey.

To those unnamed people who have trodden the same path before me, and who have freely passed on their knowledge – thank you.

To my friends and family, who have listened, talked, taught me, and borne with my sometimes-clumsy attempts to make sense of life – I love you all.

Dear Reader,

Your thoughts are your liberators and your oppressors. Your thoughts can make war or peace. Through your thoughts, anything is possible. You can make miracles . . . or you can destroy yourself. The choice is yours.

The pages in this book are my way of sharing with you my personal journey. I set out to change my life script. I felt that I'd been given such a tough one that my constant thought was not only how could I survive, but also would I survive? I was driven to find a better way.

Through meditation I saw the link between my thoughts and my actions. I realised that by taking responsibility for my thoughts I could change what was happening to me. Meditation gave me the discrimination to know which thoughts to admit as my own and which thoughts to discard. It enabled me to access the thoughts I held in my sub-conscious. I was often surprised and horrified by what was there but I persisted.

It has taken courage and humility to change my thoughts, and the process is never-ending, but it has been worth it. From a life of fight and struggle I'm making a transition to a life of acceptance and ease. I feel positive about my future.

I know that your own path is unique but I believe we have enough in common for my journey to strike a chord with you. By sharing my insights I hope you will be free to pursue the adventure that life is.

I wish you luck in your thought quest.

Greer Allica

A note on meditation

Meditation is the means to a deep inner knowing. It involves stilling the mind and body so that you can focus or reflect on one particular aspect of your life, or simply feel a part of the whole.

If your body is not calm and relaxed, it will draw your attention to it. If your mind is not still or focused, you cannot achieve peace and wisdom.

There are many ways to meditate: through breathing, through silence and non-thought, through visualisation or chanting. Meditation requires practice and dedication but it is not difficult. Find a way that suits you.

Meditation is Powerful gives insights into how, through meditation, you become aware of your thought processes so you can make your thoughts, and consequently your life, more powerful. You will find a 'thought' on one page and on the following page an exercise or reflection to take you further. The exercise can be done without meditation but it will be much more meaningful if you meditate first.

A good start to your reading on the subject of meditation might be my book *Meditation is Easy*.

A word is a seed

A word is a seed planted in the mind. It has its own energy and intent. As a small seed becomes a big and mighty tree, so the smallest word carries within itself a great power – the power to change your life and, ultimately, the world. Choose your words lovingly and nurture them as they grow into thoughts.

Seed collector

Imagine that you hold in your hand a precious and rare seed. Examine it carefully, using your five senses – hearing, seeing, taste, touch and smell. Understand what potential the seed holds. What can it become? Respect the seed and honour it with a special planting ceremony.

Jewel or dagger?

Every word you think has the potential to hurt or to heal. Words that are positive, uplifting and encouraging are like precious jewels – worth collecting and treasuring. Words that are negative, denigrating or discouraging are like a dagger in the back – they inflict wounds.

Hurt or heal?

Make a list of the healing and hurtful words
that you use. Now close your eyes and focus
firstly on the hurtful word and then on the
healing word. Repeat each word silently like a
mantra. Notice how the different words affect
you – what emotions do you feel, what body
sensations?

Inspiring words

Those who inspire with their words are leaders. They carry people with them because their words and the thoughts behind them have meaning. Inspiring words shine a light on life's path and impel people to action. Inspiring words awaken hope and banish doubt.

Taking the initiative

Don't wait for others to inspire you. Seize the initiative. How can you uplift the people around you? How can you create an environment that is uplifting? First be an example. Make every thought a loving one. Make every act an act of love.

A thoughtless word

Drop a 'thoughtless' word and it lives well beyond the second you took to say it. Thoughtless words lead to unnecessary misunderstandings. Spontaneity is a wonderful thing but if it means we hurt others, then the words we say without thinking do require some thought. Consideration of other people's sensitivities is an important part of harmonious living.

Circle of friends

Think of all your friends. What can you do to enrich your relationships? Remember that what you do is based firstly on what you think. Think of some positive, descriptive words for each of your friends. Don't just think them – say them! For example, 'I really love your sense of humour because . . .' Go into detail. Make your statement personal rather than general.

Words and thoughts

A thought is a group of connected words. Your thoughts are as important as your speech. They influence your view of the world and affect every decision and action. Every thought, expressed or unexpressed, has an effect. Don't think that by remaining silent you escape the power of your thoughts. You don't.

I think . . .

Write down ten things you think about yourself:
'I think I . . .' What do these statements reveal
about your thinking? How might others see you
if they believed these statements? Which of
these ten statements would you like to
change? Compose a 'counter-thought' for each
statement that you wish to change. Repeat the
new thought often.

Thoughts and beliefs

A belief is made up of a group of individual thoughts. Each particular thought connects or reinforces the others in the group. On its own the thought might seem harmless: for example, black is associated with death and uncleanliness. But when this statement is connected to black *people* and when other thoughts are used to support the belief, it can become dangerous. Beware of generalisations and assumptions. Beware of judgements.

Manifesto

Draw up a manifesto of your ten most important beliefs. This is the creed by which you live. Note the thoughts and then the sub-thoughts that underpin each belief. Review your manifesto. Is there anything you want to add or delete?

I think, therefore I am

What you think defines who you are, the way you appear both to yourself and to others. What you think defines your seeing, the way you select the physical realities you want to remember.

What you think defines all your outcomes. It is through your thinking that you limit or expand your world.

What is your reality?

Read any newspaper. What type of articles do you turn to? For example, do your eyes select sentences about violence and injustice to support a belief in a dangerous world? Or do you select sentences about kindness and justice to support a belief in a caring, safe world? What kind of world do you believe in? You may see only the things that support your reality.

Thoughts and speech

It is through speech that you communicate
your thoughts, but speech doesn't always
reflect the thoughts behind it. When
you say something you don't mean, you are
either unaware of your thoughts or you are
hiding them. Consciously or unconsciously
you confuse people. When feelings
conflict with thoughts you also give a mixed
message to others.

Know yourself

To know yourself you must understand what
lies beneath the surface of your street face, the
face you put on for others. When do you say
things you don't mean? Why do you do this?
Are you willing to be more honest? It is a risk
to reveal yourself but you must take that risk if
you want to be understood. Are you afraid that
you won't be accepted if you reveal who you
are? Work first on accepting yourself.

Thought energy

Every thought creates its own energy and its own momentum. The energy of a thought can uplift or depress. Be aware of where a thought or series of related thoughts will lead you. Your thoughts take you on a journey that leads to an outcome. The outcome is what you do; it is also the way others treat you. Choose what sort of energy you want to surround yourself with.

Sensing energy

Find a partner. Both close your eyes. One
partner projects thoughts to express an
emotion; for example, anger. The other senses
this emotion by sweeping one hand slowly over
their partner's body without touching it, then
describes what they feel (for example, jagged,
prickly, red, lightning). Now project thoughts
that express a contrary emotion. Change roles.

Thoughts and self-image

The thoughts you have about yourself give you a mental picture of what you are like. They define your idea of self. These thoughts are important because they affect the way you speak and look. They determine your actions and the challenges you are prepared to face. The thoughts you have about yourself also influence the **way** others see you.

This is me!

How can you summarise yourself? Here are some pointers.

'Usually I have an expression of . . . on my face.'

'Inside I often feel . . .'

'My most frequent thought is . . .'

'Compared to the people I know I am . . .'

'My greatest fear is . . .'

'Other people probably think I am . . .'

What more can you add?

Positive and negative thoughts

In everything you do you have the power to
think positively or negatively. This fact is so
very obvious that you are unlikely to give it the
consideration it deserves. Your wellbeing, your
life, hinges on how you approach every thought
and every act. Decide to live consciously and
you will make the most of your life.

Freeing your prisoner

Find one area of your life where your negative
thoughts have kept you a prisoner. Free
yourself by composing a positive thought to
match each negative one. Next time the
negative thoughts jump into your mind,
remember the positive ones you've created.
Eventually the positive will replace the negative
and a new thought pattern will begin.

Thought patterns

Thought patterns are groups of related thoughts that form a theme. They regulate and determine the way you live. They affect the way you relate to others. They can also be destructive when they lock you into a way of seeing. Your thought patterns give an insight into what motivates you. By changing your thought patterns you free yourself to explore other ways of seeing, other realities.

Finding your patterns

Look at the patterns by which you live.
Choose an area of your life you wish to change.
What are the thoughts you have made your
ground rules? Where did they come from? Are
they based on something your mother or father
said, on your relationship with your siblings?

Now you are an adult you can recognise
and *consciously* determine your thought
patterns.

Paralysing thoughts

Some thoughts paralyse – they impede action and progress, and are generated by fear. They are so powerful that they stop you living life. Every paralysing thought creates a small death within you. This type of thought is not just negative but super or ultra negative. Can you own the fear behind the thought and the fear of your fear? It is yours and you *can* do something about it.

The fear behind the thought

Look at your life. Identify where you are stuck.
Examine the thoughts you have about this area
of your life. Are they realistic or are they
controlled by fear? Do others have different
ways of coping with the same situation? How
might their thoughts also be different? Listen to
your fear and get to know it better. Recognise
that behind your fear is a frightened child.
Comfort your frightened child.

Stray thoughts

You may think that your thoughts appear from nowhere but stray thoughts don't exist. You may wonder how a particular thought got into your mind. Perhaps you are surprised by what you think. No thought appears in your conscious mind that belongs to someone else. All your thoughts belong to you. You planted them; you designed them.

Owning up

Can you be responsible for every thought
you have? Can you own the nasty, unkind
thoughts? Have you gone looking for them
or have you hidden them away? Imagine that
you are sitting on a bag of thoughts. Stand up
and open the bag. Reach for the thought
underneath the pile, at the bottom of the bag.
Meditate on this thought. Where did it begin?
Why is it there?

Unconscious thoughts

Unconscious thoughts by their very nature have a way of ruling your life. Unconscious thoughts help to determine your actions and make you feel out of control. When you feel helpless and wonder, 'How did I get into this mess?', your unconscious thoughts might be the culprits.

From unconscious to conscious

Through meditation it is possible to learn about your unconscious thoughts and bring them to the conscious mind. Breathe deeply from the diaphragm. Empty the mind of all thought, then think of a recent situation that you were unable to resolve. Replay the situation in your mind. Relive the conflict but this time with awareness. What thoughts motivated your actions?

A thought web

Your thoughts are like a web that hangs around your body. The web is an attachment that entangles or frees you. Like interconnected threads of the web, each thought is connected with others. You carry your web with you wherever you go. Look at your web of thoughts. Are you the spider whose web ensures survival and wellbeing? Or are you the fly, unaware and foolhardy, who ignores the power of the web?

Imagine . . .

. . . that you could start afresh with your thoughts. Choose the thoughts that you would like to live by. How do these thoughts connect and form their own pattern? Draw your own thought web with your name at its centre.

Unravelling a thought

- Trace your thought back to its beginning. Relate this thought to a situation you remember – the first of its kind.
- Look at parental influences. But remember, your parents are not to blame for who you are.
- Look at your recent experiences. What are you doing or thinking to reinforce your fears? What generalisations have you made from your particular experiences?

Conversation

You realise you no longer want to think the way you do about someone. Meditate on a situation associated with these unwanted thoughts. Imagine a conversation with the person involved – communicate your feelings. Question them. Why did they act the way they did? What do you want to say now that you couldn't before? Let your new understanding empower you to think differently in the future.

Group thoughts

Group thoughts have an inherent energy.
The number of people holding the same
thought magnifies its energy and makes it
especially powerful. The power can be used
for good, as in World Day of Prayer, or for bad,
as in Nazi Germany during World War II.

Group meditation

Arrange with a group of people to meditate together or individually for ten minutes on a prearranged theme. Your theme might be sending thoughts of peace and love to a country ravaged by war. You might hold an earth healing, or send thoughts of vitality and regeneration to a sick person.

Group thoughts

There are three types of group thoughts:

1. Those that belong to a certain era and are connected with a particular country or culture – for example, the twentieth century in Australia. These group thoughts provide the material for myths and legends.

2. Those that belong to movements, religions or sects – for example, hippies, Buddhists or the Amish.

3. Those that belong to individuals who all
   have the same great thoughts around the
   same time; for example, great inventors
   from different countries who have been
   working concurrently on the same ideas.
   Read about the simultaneous discovery
   of calculus by Isaac Newton and
   Gottfried Leibnitz.

Synchronicity

When thoughts occur at the same time
it is called a meaningful coincidence or
synchronicity. The theory of synchronicity
explains the connection between physical and
mental states. When the energy of one thought
is of the same frequency and pattern as the
energy of a similar thought, we talk of
synchronicity. To learn more about these
connections, read Fritjof Capra and Carl Jung
or study the theory behind the *I Ching*.

Mind reading

Have you been surprised when you have 'read' someone's mind or when a friend has contacted you at the very time you were thinking of him or her? Improve your intuitive mind by practising with a partner. Shut your eyes and relax by breathing deeply. Focus on a simple thought. Feel it, imagine it. Use all your senses to project it strongly to your partner.

Thoughts and feelings

Have you noticed the relationship between your thoughts and feelings? Your feelings are often the first indicator that something is going on in your mind. They will give you clues to your thoughts. If you are feeling miserable, you know that you are giving yourself some negative mind messages.

Feel the feeling

When you are feeling miserable you're often
tempted to push the feeling away because it is
so unpleasant. If you acknowledge the feeling
and get to know it better, you'll be able to
reach the thoughts and beliefs behind it. Close
your eyes and breathe deeply in and out from
the solar plexus, your stomach area. Feel the
feeling but don't identify with it. Remember a
part of your consciousness is the observer.

Thought, feeling and observation

Thought tends to come from the head, while feeling tends to come from the solar plexus, but both are inextricably linked. Through the sense of wholeness you achieve in meditation you can separate and look at your thoughts and feelings. You become a participant as well as an observer. Try it!

Insights

Breathe deeply till you are calm and relaxed.
Fill your mind with one thought (on an
unresolved subject) and release the others.
Now move your attention to the solar plexus
and feel the associated emotion. Observe what
is happening to you. Look carefully. Note your
new insights.

Thought mirrors

It is usually the people you are closest to
who help you to understand yourself. These
relationships can mirror your thoughts. When
someone does or says something hurtful to
you, look carefully inside yourself. Perhaps you
haven't *outwardly* attracted this treatment but
at some level you might be expecting to be
hurt. Look at your judgements and attitudes.

Transparency

Visualise light pouring in through a small hole in the crown of your head. Breathe in the light till you feel that your body is transparent. Have an attitude of surrender to your highest good, your greatest potential. Think of a relationship you want to improve. Now, as you visualise your most recent encounter with that person, observe your reaction. What are the thoughts and beliefs that drive your reaction?

Creative thoughts

Undirected thoughts that spring into your mind are often the most creative and revealing. If you want to bring on such thoughts at will, you must be relaxed and free from other distractions. Stress prevents your mind from freewheeling. Stress fills the mind with anxieties. So relax and let the thoughts flow.

Revelation

Take a sheet of paper. Write the first word that
comes into your head, then let other words
and images emerge without your mind
censoring or analysing. Doodle and draw
as well. Make it free and unplanned – not
deliberate. Finish when nothing more comes.
Now you can interpret the words and thoughts,
and the symbols in your drawing. See what
revelation appears.

Impossibility

Impossibility is an escape clause for fearful people. It begins in your mind. It is the limit you set yourself when you can't imagine a reality. Impossibility reassures you. It makes you feel safe. At the same time, the more you think things to be impossible, the more powerless you are.

Making the impossible possible

Write a sign in big letters: **Anything is possible!**
Put your sign in a prominent place and read it
often. Sing it, say it, shout it to the wind. If you
want to believe that anything is possible, you
will firstly have to convince yourself. You might
have spent a good deal of your life believing in
impossibilities, so be prepared to spend an
equal amount of time replacing that belief.

The language of possibility

Think carefully about your self-talk. If you want
things to be possible you need to say 'I can'
rather than 'I can't'. *Can* allows you to try, to
explore, to venture out. *Can* acknowledges
your self-worth, where *can't* denies it. *Can* has
a light, positive energy but *can't* is heavy and
drags you down. Say 'I can' with conviction.

The 'can' list

Write a list of all the things that you can't do
but would like to do. What is stopping you
achieving these things? Look inside yourself.
Examine your fears. Now on the other side of
the paper write your 'can' list, a list of positive
intentions. Decorate your 'can' list. Make it
your own. Continue to work on your fears so
that you *can* reclaim your personal power.

Affirming thoughts

You need to affirm yourself rather than put yourself down. If you constantly batter yourself with denigrating statements – 'You stupid fool! You're hopeless! You're an idiot!' – you become seriously incapacitated and never have the ability to recover your sense of worth. By affirming yourself you will find the courage to venture into the unknown.

Meeting the stranger

Imagine that you have an appointment with a
stranger. When you meet, the radiant presence
of this person astounds you. How can you
describe this person? What makes him or her
so special? You ask the stranger's name and
are told that you are looking at a part of
yourself. Thank the stranger and say goodbye.
Acknowledge your own inner beauty.

Think ahead

When you can already picture a situation in
the future as clearly as if it were in the present,
then you have done the necessary thought
work to make your situation real. This isn't
magic or manipulation. You are changing
yourself so that what you desire can be a
possibility. Your reality comes just as fast as
you can make it happen, as quickly as you
want to change.

Start small

Practise your visualisation skills by starting with small things you wish to achieve. Try getting yourself a parking spot right outside where you want to be. Before you arrive, see your destination clearly. Don't impose pictures on your mind. Rather, allow your consciousness to see what is already there. Sense the colours of the cars around you. Are there empty spaces? Is there a car moving out of a parking spot?

Miracles and thoughts

A miracle happens when a vision manifests itself. But a miracle is first a thought in the mind. The thought joins other thoughts to become a vision. The miracle exists as much in the thought process and the practical steps (your journey) as in its final manifestation. You are capable of a miracle if you dare to dream and to pursue your dreams.

Mapping a dream

Identify your dream. Is it realistic? Look at the
motivation behind the dream. How will you
nurture the dream so that it grows and
prospers in spite of difficulties and criticism?
What thoughts encourage or discourage the
dream's growth? What practical steps can you
take to make your dream a reality?

Unproductive thoughts

Your unproductive thoughts are those that strip you of your power. How do you get rid of a thought already implanted in your mind? Tell it to go away? That is the first step. But when the thought keeps returning as if it has a life of its own, what then? You'll need to get inside the thought. Find out what feeds the thought, what gives it life.

Free association

Free association brings to the surface the unconscious thoughts and feelings that keep you stuck. Free association also bypasses your internal censor, which protects you from change. Draw a circle in the middle of a page. Inside the circle write the thought you want to release. Focus on your thought and write down whatever comes into your mind. Connect each new thought or word with a line to the circle.

Independent thoughts

The times we live in and the people around us have a strong influence on our lives. But to what degree do you think for yourself? How easily are you swayed? Identify where you are likely to be persuaded from your viewpoint. What can you do about these vulnerable areas of your mind?

Rocks in the river

Imagine your life as a river, and the rocks as the strong and enduring thoughts in your life. Explore the rocks. What are they made of? Are your thoughts and beliefs made up of ego that has no firm base and crumbles when it is challenged?

Fiery thoughts

Fiery thoughts are the fuel for fiery words and rash action. Rage, pain and powerlessness surround such thoughts. Ego and lack of humility perpetuate rage. When you feel wounded your reaction is to strike back – you wound out of woundedness. You are caught in a vicious cycle. Your only real way out is to be courageous – stop the cycle.

Ritual burning

Replace fiery thoughts with kind thoughts. On separate pieces of paper write each angry, bitter or resentful thought. Put a match to the thoughts, one by one. Breathe out and release this way of thinking. Breathe in and rephrase the thoughts with positive, loving words. Give thanks for your new way of seeing. Remember to use your new thoughts when the next occasion arises. Nurture them.

Forgiving thoughts

Forgiveness is an act of release that involves an understanding of your own and other's actions. The act of forgiveness enables you to move on. You are no longer chained to your past. Instead, you remember it with compassion and use the wisdom you have gained to build a new future for yourself.

Setting yourself free

Spend some quiet moments setting yourself free. Visualise the person you wish to forgive. You may want to use these words or compose your own: 'I, [*your name*], totally and unconditionally forgive you, [*name of person*], for . . . Through forgiveness I release all judgement. I know that I am responsible for my present and future happiness. We are both free.'

Liberating thoughts

Liberating thoughts are those that cause
a breakthrough in your way of looking at a
situation or a person. Liberating thoughts
leave behind blame, hurt, struggle and victim
consciousness. Liberating thoughts bring a
surge of energy and exultation – they are
cause for celebration and joy. By finding joy
you get in touch with your heart.

Heart centre

As you think your liberating thoughts, focus on your heart. Feel the joy and relief of your realisation. Breathe this joy into your heart centre. With each breath draw light into your heart, with each subsequent breath feel the light radiating through your body and out through the pores of your skin. Bless the people connected with your breakthrough and thank them for the freedom you now experience.

Thoughts of the past

Your past is a sacred part of you – treat it reverently and with respect. If you deny it or repress it, your past will return to haunt you. Your past is a guide to your present. Without a past, you would have no opportunity to appraise and reflect on what you could do differently. Your present always gives you another chance to change any negative aspects of the past.

Overview

Divide your past into ages – when you were five, ten, fifteen, twenty and so on. Think of a title or summary for each age. Look back on this map of your past. What are the identifying threads of your past? What do you learn about yourself from the paths you have chosen? Look for the themes and patterns of your experience.

Thought discrimination

Unless you have a particularly strong sense of self, it is often difficult to know which thoughts belong to you and which thoughts belong to others. Doubt, fear and lack of confidence undermine and confuse you. Discrimination comes with self-awareness.

Clues

Other people give you indicators when they are
projecting their thoughts and emotions onto
you – it may be an overreaction to something
small; it may involve insistence or bullying.
Initially you will only learn about these
indicators by analysing your role and other
people's roles *after* the event. Later, you will
recognise the indicators *before* you react.
An alarm will ring in your brain. Look for
the clues . . .

Choked with thoughts

When your head spins with one thought after another, thoughts lose their power. Without this power you are unable to put your thoughts into action. Your spiritual, physical and emotional selves are out of balance. You are living in your head and you need to bring the energy back to your feet. Earth yourself by walking barefoot on the beach.

Spinning top

Imagine yourself as a spinning top. The top is your body and the energy that makes it spin is the force that propels your thoughts. Breathe out your thoughts one by one, through the top of your head. See them, still attached by their emotional content, spinning around you. Enclose them all in a balloon and set the balloon free. Watch it till it floats out of sight, then consciously release your breath.

Rearranging your thoughts

As the person in charge of your thoughts, you have the power to rearrange them in a different pattern and to bring about new understandings. You can choose linear thought (which uses the left side of the brain), where one thought progresses logically to the next, or intuitive thought (which uses the right side of the brain), where one thought connects to another through inspiration. Rearrange your thoughts by using both kinds of thinking.

Scene-changing

Write a scene from your life that involves
another person. Write it firstly in dialogue, then
from your own point of view, and then from the
other person's point of view. Finally write the
scene in the third person (he, she, it) as if you
are describing the event. What light does this
throw on your situation? How can you now
rearrange your thoughts?

Thought interpretation

Do you go through life acting as if other people are mind readers and believing that they should know how to treat you, how you think and feel? Others can only interpret you correctly if you give them correct and clear information.

Think carefully about the messages you give out and those that you neglect to give out. Are you representing yourself as truthfully and as fully as you can?

A clear message

Ways to clarity:

- define your idea
- know what belongs to you and what belongs to others
- be aware of connected emotions
- release doubts and fears.

Loving thoughts

Loving thoughts come from the heart,
unfiltered by the mind. They are without
expectation or demand. They lack judgement
and embody compassion. Loving thoughts
reach beyond ego and circumvent conflict.
They imagine harmony where none resides.
Like a scythe, love cuts through impossible
obstacles.

Heart waves

As a wave begins in a small hump, rises and gathers strength before it crashes on the shore, imagine your heart waves washing over someone you love. Focus on your heart. Feel your love grow and swell till it becomes a series of waves, then send the waves out through the power of your mind. Visualise the other person receiving your love.

A thought change

Have you heard the expression 'A change is as good as a holiday'? A thought change gives your head a rest, your mind a holiday. You can't change other people, you can't immediately change what is happening around you, but you *can* change the thoughts inside your head from heavy to light, from sad to happy, from negative to positive. These changes will energise and empower you.

Holiday

You are going on a holiday – a mind holiday.
The bags you carry with you are the thoughts
inside your head. You weigh your bags at the
airport. Remember, you can only carry so
much without a penalty. Have you given some
thought to what you carry? Have you chosen
the most suitable clothes? Are you fully
equipped for your destination?

Thinking and seeing

What you think is what you see is what you think! Think about it. A woman who becomes pregnant suddenly sees all the other pregnant women around; a person who has a broken leg suddenly sees the people with limbs in plaster; a person involved in an accident or a war suddenly becomes aware of others in a similar situation. What have you noticed in your world? How have you reinforced your observations?

Insights

Insights are lights in the darkness. The darkness is your unknowingness. The light is an area of knowing. You have seen something that was unseeable. You have made a reality from an unreality. You have changed your world.

Thought pollution

You harm your body and mind by the
poisonous thoughts that you hang onto over
time. Poisonous thoughts are those that
damage your wellbeing or anyone else's.
Thought pollution is as dangerous as the
deadliest chemical. You can't let someone else
clean up your own mind, because only you
know what's in it. Look at the consequences of
the negative thoughts you hold. How do they
spoil every other thought?

A mental spring-clean

Begin by noticing the thoughts that are harmful. Take one at a time – don't overload yourself. Identify the harmful aspects and the person or people involved. Can you communicate with them (in reality or through meditation) and acknowledge what you have been thinking? After you have laid bare your mental environment, think about how you will replant it.

Painful thoughts

Painful thoughts often originate from painful memories. The memories are constantly reinforced by present situations. You *expect* that something painful will occur because it did in the past. Now you find it difficult to alter the painful thoughts because they appear even before the situation has manifested. You are stuck in a vicious cycle.

Re-imaging

Replace the negative picture you have built up
in your mind by creating a new image to
overlay the old one. Imagine the situation the
way you would like it to be. See it, hear it, feel
it, sense it. Know it. Through your imagination
you open the door of possibility where before it
was barred. You believe that things can be
different.

Thought shields

Thought shields are the mind's rational defence mechanisms – the excuses for not changing. Thought shields are masks. They keep your fears intact and protect you from experience. They reassure you and make you feel safe but in fact they more often put limits around your life. If your thought shields are strong you never move beyond your comfort zone. You stop growing.

Disarming

Make a list of some of your thought shields, then release them one by one. Visualise yourself dressed in armour on the battlefield. Your armour is punctured. An 'enemy' approaches and removes your shield. What insights are you left with? Who does the 'enemy' represent? How did *you* create the 'battle'?

Thought protection

You can use your mind to protect you from harmful situations – when negative people sap your energy, when you are stressed, when you empathise too strongly with those you love. Use your mind to separate your thoughts and feelings from those around you.

Circle of light

Imagine that you have X-ray vision and can see the energy around the surface of your body. Is the energy dense or light? Is it composed of dull, muddy colours or bright, clean colours? Feel it, see it – use your X-ray vision. Now create a circle of light around your body (breathe in the light) and see the area become clear.

Changing the world

You have within you the tools to change not only yourself, but also the world in which you live. You might think that you can do little to change the world, but your role is crucial. Through your thoughts you create a setting for right action. Right action is motivated by love and the absence of harm. Right action works for the good of all.

Trouble spots

Take your consciousness to the trouble spots
of the world. Imagine peace replacing war.
Peace is an abstract concept but you can
make it live in your mind by visualising the
effects of peace. How do people look when
they are peaceful? How do they behave
towards one another? See it, feel it. Make
your imagined scene so real that it lives.

A state of bliss

Do you look at other people and envy their happiness? Happiness is not a result of what you possess but a state of mind. Bliss begins with thankfulness and an acceptance of the nature of change. Everything changes. Nothing stays. You can't hold onto anything in life. Bless what comes to you – you are constantly *be*coming.

Letting go

If you hang onto the idea of happiness it slips out of reach. Look carefully at your definitions of happiness and the way you have let these ideas govern your life. What are the ideas based on? How can you loosen their hold over you? What have you made permanent and unchanging and how does it imprison you?

Jumping to conclusions

Your mind plays tricks on you. It takes you
from one thought to the next and all of a
sudden you have a central and conclusive
thought that is stuck in your brain with no
intention of going away. Your conclusion
appears obvious and unavoidable. The
thoughts that led to your conclusion seemed
like a straight path, but check the route.
You'll be surprised.

Check your thoughts

When you come to a conclusion at lightning speed or when your conclusion is rock solid, it's time to check your thoughts. How did you get to this point? Look at your emotions – what are you protecting, doubting, fearing? How do you feel about what you are thinking? Look at the interplay between yourself and other people. Know what thoughts belong to you and why they are there.

Just thoughts

Just thoughts are the opposite of rash thoughts. They come from coolness, not from fire. They come from a rational, considered mind that is tempered with compassion and kindness. *Just* thoughts are the prelude to *just* words and *justice*.

The judge

You are your own best and worst judge. You are the dispenser of justice to yourself and to others. If you are kind and compassionate with yourself, you'll be the same with others. If you are unjust and harsh with yourself, you will be judgemental towards others.

Bold thoughts

Bold thoughts are brave thoughts. They are like an open window in the mind. They are a fresh wind in a room of stale air. They dare to be different, to explore, to challenge. Bold thoughts need a strong base or they will be dashed down at the hint of opposition.

The courage to be bold

How would you be if you had the courage to be bold? Take the risk. Make a list of bold intentions for yourself, noting the idea, associated thoughts and action. For example: 'If I were courageous I would be . . . able to speak confidently in front of large groups'.

Associated thoughts: replace the negative (your mental block) with the positive – 'People think I'm stupid' becomes 'People accept me as I am'. Associated action: enrol in a public speaking course.

The persuader

In any group there is always a person with
a gift for words, one who paints such a
wonderful word picture that others are swayed.
If you are the persuader think about your
motivation. Is it your intention to manipulate
or to inspire? Is your intention selfish or is it
motivated by love? If you are one of the group,
ask yourself, 'Am I being true to myself if
I follow this person's advice?'

A point of view

Think of something that you want to communicate to others. Form a clear picture of the underlying thoughts to your topic – why it's important to you; how it's connected with your past, your feelings; why you want to communicate with these particular people. Rehearse in front of the mirror. Notice how you are most persuasive when your body, your mind and your emotions are all working together with a clear aim.

Leaders and followers

It's much easier to follow than to lead. Leaders are prepared to air their thoughts in public and to risk ridicule. A follower has often not put in the mental work required to bring about an action. There may be many reasons for this – shyness, fear, feelings of incompetence, inferiority. Don't be afraid to look at these reasons, if they are relevant.

Sending messages

You have an important message that you want someone or others to hear. What mental weapons do you need to prepare yourself? Visualise yourself going into 'battle'. You are a warrior on a personal crusade to be heard. How are you hindered in your quest? Look carefully at the symbols that appear. They represent the thoughts, abilities, attitudes and actions you need to get your message across.

Thoughts and actions

Every action has a thought behind it. We talk about a person behaving thoughtlessly and about a thoughtless act, but what we really mean is that the thought was mismatched with the act, and only in someone's opinion. The act may have come from an unconscious thought or feeling. Or it may have resulted from a mixture of competing thoughts.

Tracing back

Remember a recent occasion when what you
did caused an unexpected reaction from
another person. Meditate. Re-imagine the
occasion, using all your senses to make it real.
This time, as well as being the participant, be
the observer. What do you notice about your
words, your appearance, your feelings?
Observe the other person closely too. Perhaps
this time you can talk to them. Ask questions.
Listen for the answers.

Imaginary thoughts

When you go through a number of bad experiences with someone it is easy to establish a destructive thought pattern, where you use your thoughts to verify and reinforce your bad experiences. You set up imaginary scenarios for the next bad experience. You become the imaginary mouthpiece of your 'opponent'.

Getting in touch

Take charge of your own thoughts instead of
taking charge of someone else's through your
imagination. Look at *your* part. Reflect on what
is happening. Look for patterns or common
responses. Then meditate on the experience –
be especially aware of your feelings and where
the feeling is located in your body. What is
behind the feeling? Where does it come from?

Demeaning thoughts

Demeaning thoughts arise from a lack of
self-worth (and tap into another's lack of self-
worth) – there is a need to put someone down
so that you can elevate yourself. The person
who demeans feels threatened and fearful. As
the word implies, such thoughts are mean and
petty. In order to exist, these thoughts need
competition and comparison.

Looking past the insult

The next time people try to put you down, mentally refuse to connect. Remember that their words come from *their* insufficiency, not yours. Imagine them as tame pussycats! You are bending over them, tickling their tummies, giving them the attention and love that they need.

Scattered thoughts . . .

. . . are seeds tossed by the wind. They have no direction or discipline and fall unused among the chaff. When scattered thoughts dominate your mind, ask yourself, 'What am I avoiding?'

Winnowing . . .

. . . is the process of sorting the seed from the chaff. It is discernment. Imagine you are standing in the middle of a field. You have a pocketful of seed thoughts. Run your hand through the seeds. Select the one you want to plant. What is it called? Breathe the thought into your body till it is planted deep in the core of your being. Let loose the other seeds to the wind.

Lazy thinking

When a thought is half thought it has no base,
no resting place. It languishes and dies. Its
potential is lost. Have you the willpower to
pursue the adventure of your thought?

Cultivating willpower

- Try again – don't give up at the first sign of difficulty.
- Be prepared for and able to deal with criticism.
- Remember you are in charge of your thoughts – you're free to choose them, free to change them.
- Know where you want to go and go there willingly.

Food for thought

The food you eat (and the amount) affects
both body *and* mind. Drugs cloud the mind.
A healthy, balanced diet with lots of water,
fresh fruit and vegetables, grains and a little
meat, if desired, ensures an alert mind.

Brain foods

- B vitamins – for the nervous system.
- Antioxidants – to protect nerve cells and reduce free radicals, which damage cell structure. Take vitamin E or green tea.
- Phosphatidyl choline (found in lecithin) – to help concentration.
- Ginkgo biloba and rosemary – for memory.
- Ginseng – for stress and mental strength.

Thoughts feed the body

Positive, uplifting, joyful thoughts have a beneficial effect on the body. Your thoughts and the connecting emotions bring about chemical reactions that change every cell in your body. As each cell constantly renews itself, it is never too late to make healthy cells by changing the thoughts that you hold in your mind.

Body beautiful

Use your mind to channel light into each cell
of your body. Visualise the light penetrating
and enlivening. See the organs as vibrant and
healthy. Give thanks to each part of your body,
each organ for the wonderful job it does.

Thankful thoughts . . .

. . . are re*mind*er notes that ensure you take nothing for granted, that life doesn't pass by without you noticing. To live life your mind must participate and engage with it. Thankful thoughts are a silent communication with the giver.

Support network

Think of your family, friends, mentors, heroes and heroines. How have they each helped and supported you? Mentally send them thanks. Now give thanks to those unknown people in positions of power and authority who also affect the way you live.

Vain thoughts . . .

. . . are driven by an insecure ego and a self-conscious view of life. Instead of flowing with life, you've created a fixed image for yourself. You compare yourself with others. Your mind specialises in imposed standards and is governed by 'shoulds' – 'I should be . . .'

Good enough

Relax! You are *already* good enough. You cannot be compared with unless you permit it to happen. Believe in your own uniqueness and your ability to become whoever you want to be. You don't need to justify your being. You just *are* . . . and that is okay.

Humorous thoughts . . .

. . . take the struggle out of life. They help you walk on water and fly through the air because living is light and anything is possible. Through humour you make yourself indestructible. You have the courage to make life an adventure. Nothing daunts you.

Clown face

Put on your clown face and bumble into
catastrophe. Imagine you are the clown in your
daunting situation. See how much slapstick
humour you can inject into your act. Notice
the surprised faces in the audience. Now use
your 'clown' in the real situation.

Wishful thinking . . .

. . . is wishy-washy thinking. It is enfeebling, and an excuse for staying where you are and letting others achieve your dreams. Wishful thinkers work with the premise: 'If only . . .' Take a mental hold on your wishes and do something with them.

Working with a wish

Look at your wish. Is it realistic? To realise
a wish you must journey towards it. Each step
of your journey brings you closer to your
destination. Map out the steps as far as you
can see. Have faith that the others will unfold
when you have had the courage to begin.
What skills and personal qualities do you have
that will help you along your way?

Pollyanna thoughts . . .

. . . are positive thoughts with no depth. They are built of sand and crumble away at the first challenge of the tide. Positivity has strength and endurance when it encounters and understands the negative.

Falsely positive

Look at your 'positive' thoughts. Identify those without a stable foundation. What have you glossed over? Find your shadow self – the self you would rather not know – and get to know it better. Your shadow self is the spider in the cupboard. It will crawl out and surprise you if you don't find it first by opening the cupboard.

Thoughts and consequences

Thoughts *do* have consequences. You are a wise person if you can see the consequences *before* you have expressed your thoughts or acted upon them. Consequences may be far-reaching – they might limit or enrich your life.

Projecting forward

In order to see consequences you need to take a mental journey into the future. Select a thought. What other thoughts are dependent on this central one? How might each of these thoughts influence your actions? Visualise yourself in the situation where your thought has taken you. Do you feel comfortable? What details do you need to alter?

Fearful thoughts

Don't be ashamed of your fearful thoughts.
Everybody is fearful at times. Fear is a
protection and, initially, it serves a purpose, to
protect you from situations you are not ready
to handle. Ask yourself, 'Does my fear help or
hinder me?' Be honest. Keep reviewing your
fearful thoughts. Check when they have
passed their use-by date.

Your worst fear

What is your worst fear? Look at the ways in which it has protected you: 'This fear has helped me to . . .' Look at the ways in which it has limited you: 'This fear has stopped me believing in . . . This fear has stopped me doing . . .'

Generous thoughts . . .

. . . give others the benefit of your doubt.
Generous thoughts say 'no' to fear. They
encourage your 'good' and mentally prepare
you to bring abundance into your life. Generous
thoughts are woven from compassion and an
understanding that we are all human and that
we all make mistakes. Most people don't
intentionally set out to hurt others.

Spare a thought . . .

. . . for your 'enemy', the person you like most to hate, the person for whom you can't find a good word. Imagine you are meeting them face-to-face to express your thoughts. Look carefully. Listen carefully. What is the reply? Now take each other's hands and compose your one generous thought. With your mind's focus on your heart, express this thought. Feel it. Look into your 'enemy's' eyes.

Trusting thoughts

Trust is a leap of faith, though it sometimes feels like a leap in the dark. It is really a leap from an enlightened attitude that assumes the best of people and believes that everyone is capable of change. To be let down once or twice doesn't *necessarily* mean that it will happen again.

The cliff jump

Imagine you are standing on the edge of a cliff looking across a chasm to someone on the other side. 'Jump and I'll catch you,' the person calls. What thoughts do you need now in order to trust and make the jump? On a beam of light send your trusting thoughts across the chasm. Now jump and propel yourself through the shaft of light.

Sympathetic thoughts . . .

. . . arise from compassion and the knowledge that each of us is unique. Sympathy is the act of stepping into someone's emotional field without being swamped. Put your own feelings, judgements and solutions aside so you can listen and then imagine what the other person is going through.

Suspending judgement

Look at your thoughts the next time you're faced with a tale of woe. What sprang into your mind? Did you want to judge or rescue? Were you angry or withdrawn? Try to separate the feelings and thoughts that belong to you. What sympathetic thoughts *could* you have had? Rehearse them.

Alienating thoughts . . .

. . . come from an exaggerated idea of difference and a fear that you won't be understood or accepted for who you are. Look for the features that unite rather than divide and at the same time accept that you are uniquely *you*, and that is okay. When you feel that nobody understands you, think how you can reach out and communicate.

Unmasking

Imagine you are at the centre of a circle that holds all the difficult people you know. Shut your eyes and feel what it is like to be here. When you open your eyes, you notice that each person has a mask. Approach everyone in the circle and remove the masks. What thoughts keep the masks in place?
What thoughts are behind the masks?

Thoughts and reality

Look around you and you'll see not one world
but many. There are worlds within worlds and
it is through your thoughts that you construct
your reality. Whatever you notice (see, hear,
touch, feel, taste) becomes real to you. What
you fail to notice becomes non-existent – you
don't know about it. You can change your
reality by deciding to look for the unknown.

A reality check

What worlds do your friends and family
inhabit? Look at the words they speak and the
ways they act. If you can understand and map
their reality it will help you to guess the areas
they can't 'see'. How have you altered the
thought patterns you grew up with?

Thought and intention

Thoughts form an intention when they
are focused and clear. When thoughts
become scrambled the intention is lost and
misunderstandings result. You say, 'It
isn't what I intended,' because you have
conflicting thoughts and feelings.

Misunderstandings

Look at some of your misunderstandings with others. Were you aware of your intentions in the communication? Were there many intentions? Look at the gap between what you wanted to say and what you did say. Be honest with yourself. What was motivating you?

Owning your thoughts

It might seem obvious to say 'Your thoughts belong to you', but consider what it means. It means you can no longer think as if it doesn't matter *what* you think. You can no longer believe that as long as you don't speak your thoughts it doesn't matter. You can no longer believe that there are no consequences to the thoughts you have.

Resolution

Make a resolution: 'From now on I will lovingly nurture my thoughts because they are the origin of my personal expression. I will take responsibility for every thought I have. I will be aware of my self-talk and of how I communicate with others. Through my thoughts I will become a more beautiful person'.

About the author

Change and expression have been central themes of Greer Allica's life . . .

A graduate of the University of Melbourne with English and Political Science majors, and a sub-major in Indian Studies, she later studied philosophy, different religions, psychology, mind dynamics, therapeutic and remedial massage, yoga, reiki and spiritual healing. Greer has been a teacher, librarian, masseuse, counsellor, and meditation and yoga teacher. She has a passion for travel, other cultures and languages.

Greer is the author of *Meditation is Easy*, *Easy Steps to Healing* and *Meditation Workbook*.